HOW TO PAINT
PORTRAITS
IN OIL

Macdonald

HOW TO USE THIS BOOK

Here are step-by-step demonstrations of a range of subjects in different media, designed specially to show you how to paint and draw portraits. To get the most out of these exercises, study each one first and then either re-draw or re-paint it yourself or, using the same medium, apply the same techniques to your own subject.

Copying. Don't be concerned about the fact that you are copying these exercises — many famous artists have used other artists' ideas and painting techniques to develop their own unique style. And copying the exercises will make learning the techniques easier for you as you won't have to worry about finding a subject, composition or design.

Stay loose. It is best to attack each project vigorously, and aim to make a strong painting. Don't worry about making mistakes along the way — the more you practise and experiment, the quicker and more dramatic will be your improvement in painting.

Experiment. By working boldly and taking risks with lines, colour, shapes and values, you will avoid the risk of your pictures looking tight and overworked. When you are making broad, generous strokes, don't hold your pencil or brush too near the point or your lines and brushwork will look tentative. Only when working on detail should you hold your brush or pencil close to the point — and keep your details to minimum when beginning a drawing or painting. Usually they are best left for the finishing touches.

Keep it simple. Select simple poses compositions to start with. Restrict yourself to a simple range of colours, and keep these crisp and pure by taking care not to overwork or smudge them on the canvas or paper.

If you observe these basic points, you will quickly produce surprisingly good paintings and then you can really start to experiment with bolder composition, more vibrant or subtle colour schemes, and develop your unique painting style.

Happy painting!

Contributing artists: pp 4-9, 16-21, Stan Smith;
pp 10-15, 22-27, 28-30, Ian Sidaway

A MACDONALD BOOK

© Quintet Publishing Ltd 1987

First published in Great Britain in 1986
by Macdonald & Co (Publishers) Ltd
London & Sydney

A member of BPCC plc

How to paint portraits in oils.
The Macdonald Academy of Art
1. Portrait painting — Technique
I. Series
751.45'42   ND1302

ISBN 0-356-12349-9

This book was designed and produced by
Quintet Publishing Limited
6 Blundell Street, London N7

Typeset in Great Britain by
Facsimile Graphics Limited, Essex
Colour origination in Hong Kong by
Hong Kong Graphic Arts Limited, Hong Kong
Printed in Hong Kong by Leefung-Asco
Printers Limited

CONTENTS

If you have not painted in oils before you will need to buy some simple equipment. It will be cheaper to buy the items separately rather than as a ready-made set. You only need a few colours to start with — you can mix other colours from the basic palette. Start with titanium white, ivory black, cobalt blue, yellow ochre, viridian, raw umber and cadmium red. Other useful colours are French ultramarine, burnt Sienna, alizarin crimson, terre verte (a translucent green earth colour which is useful for portraits) and cadmium yellow. There are two ranges of oil paint: Student's colours are the cheapest and are adequate for most purposes; Artist's colours are more expensive because the pigments are purer and there is a greater range of colours. You will need turpentine to dilute your paint, white spirit for cleaning your brushes and some linseed oil. Oil painting brushes are usually made from bleached hog's hair or red sable. Hog's hair are used for most purposes though red sable brushes are useful for detailed work as they are usually smaller and thinner. Brushes are expensive and should be treated with care. Always clean them after use. Finally, you will need a suitably prepared painting surface — hardboard primed with an acrylic primer is cheap and you can use the smooth or the textured side. Oil sketching paper, and prepared boards can be bought from any art supply shop. Prepared canvases are expensive but you can buy canvas and stretchers and prepare your own quite cheaply and simply.

INTRODUCTION

History of portraiture

The art of portraiture has passed in and out of favour throughout history. The Greeks produced some of the most beautiful representations of mankind ever, but the sculptors and painters of Ancient Greece were concerned with representing ideal rather than realistic images. The Greek passion for the ideal obliterated personality; a man who is truly perfect loses those characteristics which make him an individual. The Romans on the other hand produced portraits which were often unflattering and sometimes brutal in the realism with which the subjects were depicted. In A.D. 311 the Roman Emperor Constantine I proclaimed Christianity the offical religion of his state — a decision which had a profound effect on the art of the Western world. Secular art was proscribed and only subjects with a religious message were allowed. Portraits of donors were sometimes included in paintings but generally the art of portraiture went into a decline until it was revived during the Renaissance when it achieved an importance it has held fairly consistently ever since.

Approaches to the portrait

Artists vary in their approach for some the presentation of the personality of their subjects is important — this has sometimes cost them their reputations and the support of wealthy patrons. Artists who can achieve good likenesses have usually been able to earn a living by recording their clients as they would wish to be portrayed, in moments of triumph, dressed in their robes of office or surrounded by evidence of their power and wealth.

Achieving a 'likeness'

A 'good likeness' implies that the sum of the features is instantly recognisable to anyone who has met or seen the subject. And it is generally assumed that all the greatest portrait painters were able to oblige their patrons with such a likeness. But the artist does not necessarily reveal much about the character of the subject by merely reproducing the features of the sitter. No portrait is objective for it is a record of how one person sees another — some are sympathetic, others cold and formal, others are satirical. A portrait may, in fact, tell us more about the artist and the relationship betweeen the artist and the sitter than it does about the subject.

The underlying structure

The skull provides the basic framework for the head — its shape defines its structure and the bones provide the anchorage points for the muscles. The skull is divided into two main components — the cranium which protects the brain and the facial bones which define the features of the face. There are 28 bones in the human head and all except the jawbone are firmly attached to each other.

At birth the head forms a greater proportion of the total body length than in adults and the cranium in turn occupies a larger proportion of the volume of the head. The cranium is composed of thin curved plates which in the new born are separated by fibrous tissue at their edges. In the first years of life the bones grow and fuse together to form a rigid protective casing. The skull of an infant differs from that of an adult and much of the excess tissue around the cheeks camouflages the facial bone

Above An English Lady by Hans Holbein (1497–1543). This was a study for a group portrait of the family of Sir Thomas More. The woman is thought to be Margaret Roper, one of More's daughters. Holbein's method was to make meticulous drawings from life and to use these drawings as the basis of a painting.

structure which will become more prominent as time goes by. With old age the skin tends to lose its elasticity and sags so the bones appear to be nearer the surface. The degree to which a person's bone structure can be seen depends on factors such as sex, age and racial origin.

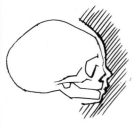

These three skull diagrams show some of the changes that occur in the face between infancy and old age. In the first **(above)** *— showing the head of a young child — the upper part of the head is large and long in relation to the face. Notice the jaw which is hardly developed at all.*

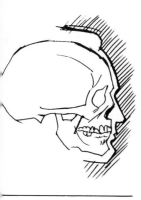

With the growth of teeth and the strengthening of the jaw-bones, the face lengthens and the forehead becomes more prominent **(above)** *so that in the adult there is less difference in size between the face and the skull.*

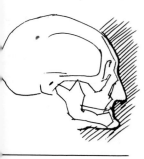

In old age, teeth are lost, the skin loses its elasticity, and muscles waste so that the features of the face tend to droop and the bones of the skull become more prominent. It is important to be aware of the shape of the underlying bone structure when drawing or painting faces of any age.

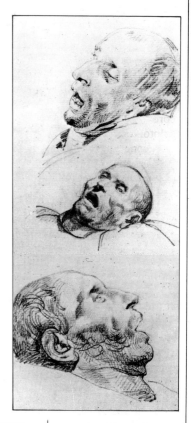

Above left Self Portrait, *by Peter Paul Rubens (1577–1640). Rubens was a gifted draughtsman and a wonderful colourist. Like Rembrandt and many other artists he painted his own face several times. These paintings and drawings are exercises in capturing emotions and expressions.*

Above *Théodore Géricault's studies for* The Raft of Medusa *reflects the artist's impassioned reaction to the aftermath of the shipwreck. The faces express both fear and loss.*
Left *By contrast, a modern artist has captured the innocence of youth in this sketch of a sleeping child.*

PORTRAIT OF A YOUNG GIRL

In this painting the artist is concerned with the effect of light on the model, the way it illuminates and describes the form and at the same time dissolves it into strange and abstract shapes and facets. The way in which a subject is lit can affect a painting in many ways. Light can change the mood of a painting and also influences the colours which can be perceived. Notice the way in which the finished painting dissolves into patterns of light and shade as you approach — it only really 'reads' when viewed from a considerable distance.

One of the most important and most difficult aspects of portrait painting is achieving good skin tones. The colour of skin varies enormously depending on race, age and even on the amount of sun you have been exposed to. Many experienced painters have a formula for achieving good flesh tones and you will undoubtedly evolve

your own. A word of warning — the commercially available paints called 'flesh' are sadly misnamed. Some are actually a bright salmon pink, so don't think you have found the easy way out when you come across one in your local artist's supply shop.

The best way to paint flesh it to look carefully at the subject and paint what you see. Work cooler colours into your shadow areas and warm colours onto the highlighted areas on the cheek, forehead and nose. Apply the paint lightly and freely, working wet-into-wet as the artist has done here, or laying down patches of pre-mixed colours — a method used in some of the other paintings in this book. An overworked paint surface can 'kill' a portrait more surely than any other subject — skin must look fresh and living to be convincing.

*The artist spends a considerable time considering the pose. He sits the model (**far left**) so that the light falls on her from the window on the right. Because the light source is natural the artist has to work quickly in order to get as much of the painting down on canvas as possible, before the light changes. He works on the picture over several days, returning to it at the same time of day so that the light conditions are almost constant.*

*The artist selects a fine grained prepared board (24 x 30 in). Using cobalt blue thinly diluted with turpentine he starts to draw in the main outlines of the head. Notice the way in which he marks the line of the nose and the chin, the horizontal which runs through the eyes and the left side of the nose (**left**).*

*Using the same washy paint and a no 5 flat bristle brush he starts to block in the shadow areas. At this stage he is not concerned with the details of the head. He concentrates on the broad areas of light and dark and the forms emerge very quickly (**left** and **below**).*

*Using a rag the artist smudges in some areas of tone to indicate the shadow behind the model (**left**). The rag can also be used to correct the drawing where necessary.*

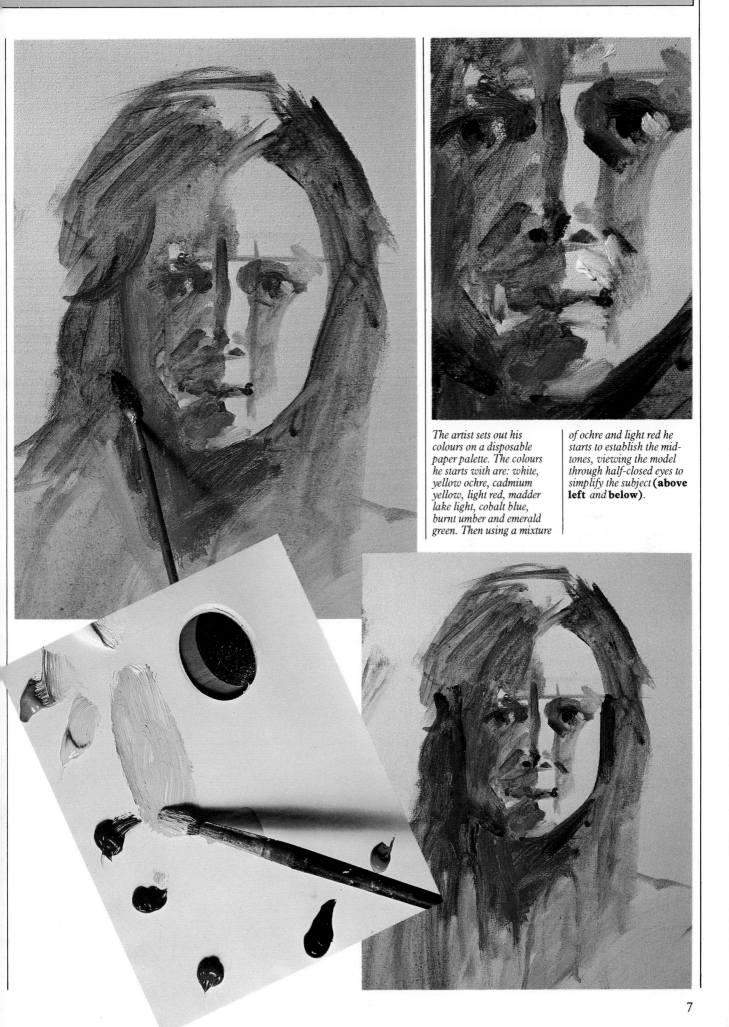

The artist sets out his colours on a disposable paper palette. The colours he starts with are: white, yellow ochre, cadmium yellow, light red, madder lake light, cobalt blue, burnt umber and emerald green. Then using a mixture of ochre and light red he starts to establish the mid-tones, viewing the model through half-closed eyes to simplify the subject (**above left** and **below**).

As you can see from the details on this page, at this stage the artist has actually put very little paint on the canvas and yet the image is already beginning to emerge and is clearly recognizable as the model. He continues to work in broad areas and planes of lighter and darker colours, avoiding the temptation to concentrate on minute details. If you find that the forms of the features have begun to get lost under layers of paint you can redefine or redraw the features with a fine brush.

The artist is using a large (no 10) bristle brush. By using a brush which is a size larger than you feel comfortable with, you will force yourself to work broadly and this too will stop you fiddling with the paint. One of the pleasures of oil paint is the quality of the paint, its manoeuverability, its flexibility and the way in which you can change it, move it and overpaint it. But this very flexibility may seduce you into playing with the paint too much so that your paint loses its freshness and your colours become muddy.

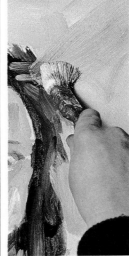

In the details **top left** and **top right** the artist has developed the details of the face. Notice the darker tones under the lower lip and nose, and the way in which these small areas of darker tone help to bring out the three-dimensionality of the face. The artist has created emphasis around the eyes but has avoided the temptation to 'draw' the eye, a common mistake among less experienced painters.

The hair is described using a mixture of light red and burnt umber. This is laid on thinly and the artist then works into it with yellow and ochres to establish the highlights where the hair catches the light.

In the details at the **bottom** of the page the artist is using a small household paint brush to cover the background and the broad areas of the girl's blouse. It is useful to establish these background areas quickly as it allows you to judge your colours against each other, rather than against the white ground.

At this stage the model was allowed to rest!

9

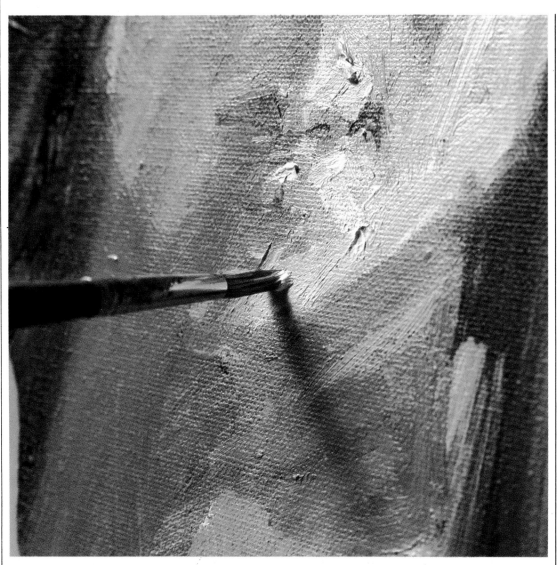

*In the details (**left** and **below left**) we can see the way in which the texture of the canvas animates the painting. In places the artist has allowed the canvas and the original drawing to show through, adding a lively sparkle to the finished painting. Do not feel that you must entirely cover the canvas before you can consider the painting 'finished'. In the detail (**above**) the artist uses a small brush to add highlights to the area under the brow and the upper eyelid, still resisting the temptation to draw the eyes.*

The final picture is a lively and colourful likeness of the sitter. The artist could have taken it further, but would have risked losing the immediacy which characterised the painting. One of the most difficult decisions for an artist is deciding when a painting is 'finished'.

WOMAN IN A BLACK SLIP

The artist has chosen an unusual pose with the model's head turned away from the viewer. The painting is nevertheless an acute and penetrating portrait of the subject, instantly recognisable to those who know her. We recognise our friends by the way they move, the postures they adopt and by their facial features. The back view can often say as much as the more usual frontal or three-quarters view.

The composition is simple, with the figure silhouetted against the pale and uncluttered background, creating a pattern of bold forms which work one against the other. The spaces between the elements of a painting are an important part of the composition. These spaces known as 'negative spaces' create a second level of interest — an underlying abstract pattern.

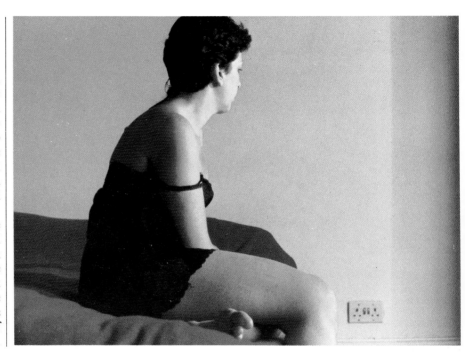

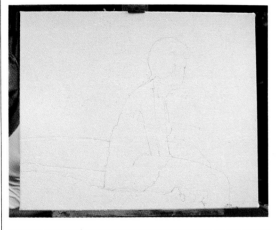

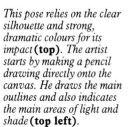

*This pose relies on the clear silhouette and strong, dramatic colours for its impact (**top**). The artist starts by making a pencil drawing directly onto the canvas. He draws the main outlines and also indicates the main areas of light and shade (**top left**).*

*Using flat black paint the artist lays in the hair of the model (**centre right**), leaving patches of white canvas to stand for the highlights (**far left**). He mixes a darker skin tone and starts to paint the shaded side of the figure (**left**), leaving the lighter areas.*

The artist continues to lay in the darker skin tones **(below)**. He then mixes a light flesh tone by adding a little white to the colour he has already mixed. He proceeds to lay in this colour. In the detail **(right)** you can see the way in which the colour has been laid down in discrete areas of flat colour which abut upon each other with clearly defined edges. These sharp edges dissolve as you move away from the painting so that the eye sees only modulated tones, lighter where the light catches the figure and darker where the figure is turned away **(above)**.

The artist is working with fairly fluid paint thinly diluted with turpentine. He uses a small, soft, synthetic fibre brush for working into the areas of fine detail. He continues to work across the whole figure, dividing the skin tones into areas of lights and darks **(left)**. His approach contrasts with the loosely worked paint and rich impastos of the previous portrait.

In the detail **(left)** he adds black and raw umber to the skin tones to obtain a dark brown for the very darkest areas. Notice the way in which the texture of the canvas shows through the thin paint layer, acting as a unifying factor throughout the painting.

Oil paint is a very flexible medium and the paint can be handled in a variety of ways, from thick impastos to thin glazes. In the previous painting the artist mixed his colours on the palette and also slurred colours together on the canvas to create a new colour. Here the artist mixes each colour on his palette, and then applies the colour, without further mixing.

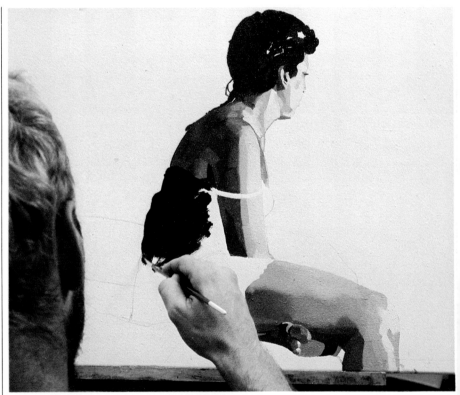

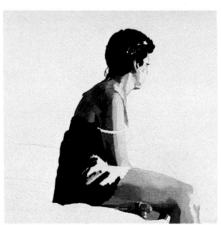

Using pure black paint, the artist starts to lay in the black underslip (**centre left** and **right**). He leaves the highlight areas white, ready to receive the lighter tone later (**above**).

Now the artist mixes a creamy colour using white and raw umber and with this starts to lay in the background. The paint is fluid and does not hold the marks of the brush, creating areas of matt, untextured colour (**left**).

He continues to work into the background, using a small brush to create the complicated contours of the figure **(above)**.

In the detail on the **left** the artist is using a mixture of cadmium red deep and raw umber to describe the shadow areas of the red coverlet. He uses several shades of one colour to establish the lights and darks — here, on the body of the model and even on her slip. He matches the pigment to the colour of the subject as closely as possible, before putting it on the canvas. Other artists take a close equivalent of the colour and lighten or darken it on the canvas. Remember that colours are modified by surrounding colours so that a colour which looked right on the palette may look wrong when it is laid on the canvas.

15

This painting illustrates the way in which subtly varied tones, applied in small, flat areas of colour, combine to create a solid, three-dimensional form on the canvas (**left**). The limbs have a convincingly rounded quality because the skin tones change gradually from light to dark across the form, as the quantity of light reflected changes (**below left** and **right**).

In the picture (**bottom right**) the artist uses pure cadmium red to add a final exciting touch of colour.

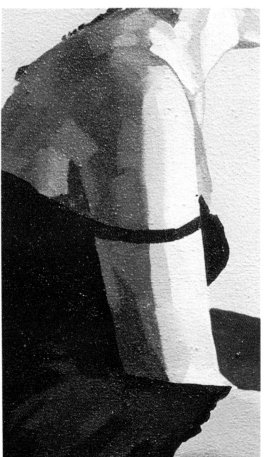

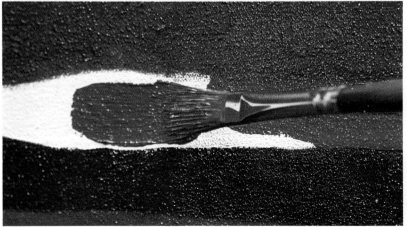

In the final picture we see the way in which the artist has let the white of the canvas stand for the highlight areas where the most direct light is striking the figure. He has worked up to the area of light, painting the darks and the mid-tones so that the higlight areas are established by a process of elimination — they are where the dark is not. He has 'felt' the shapes and volumes of the figure and has created an image which has both bulk and weight. The painting is also a pleasing abstract pattern, the areas of red and black creating interesting patterns against the relatively empty background.

A SELF-PORTRAIT

An artist is often his or her own best model — no other model will ever be so patient, so readily available or so cheap. Most of the great artists have painted self-portraits during their career. Rembrandt painted a series throughout his life and they are a wonderful record of his development as a man and as an artist.

Setting up a self-portrait is important. Make sure that you have a mirror in which you can easily see yourself without twisting or stretching. You should be able to look from the canvas to the mirror merely by shifting your gaze. Ensure that you have an adequate light source — it can be artificial or natural. The light should be sufficient to see by but it should also add interest to the painting. Make sure that you can reach all your materials easily and don't forget to

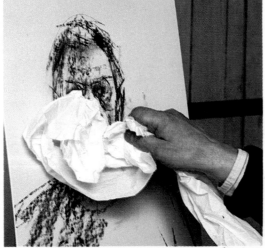

*Here the artist has used charcoal to establish the broad outlines of the subject. He has used line to set out the main structures and has used the side of the stick to lay in broad areas of tone. Charcoal is soft and dusty and the black powder will contaminate any paint you lay over it unless it is fixed. Alternatively, you can use the method shown **above** and **right** which is to brush off the surface powder by flicking it with a duster. You can re-establish the lines of the drawing at this stage by tracing over them with paint.*

mark the position of the easel, the mirror and your feet so that when you step back or leave the painting for any period of time you will be able to resume the position and pose again.

The artist started by making a fairly detailed underdrawing using charcoal. The degree of detail in the underdrawing depends on the method of working of the artist. Some produce a very sketchy underdrawing and work up the details in paint; others, as in this case, use the drawing to work out aspects of the composition such as the distribution of the tonal areas.

The artist's approach was simple and direct. He painted what he saw, concentrating on tones and shapes but has nevertheless achieved an excellent likeness.

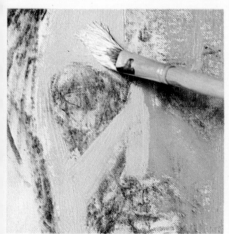

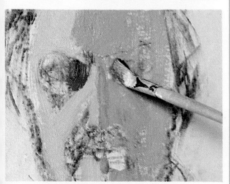

*The artist starts by laying out his initial palette of cadmium red, cobalt, burnt umber, burnt sienna, yellow ochre and white (**top**). He will add other colours as the painting progresses. Next he mixes some flesh tints using combinations of ochre, white and burnt sienna for the warmer tints adding cobalt for the cooler tints. With quite thin paint he starts to block in the main tonal areas of the face, identifying the subtle changes by peering at his image in the mirror through half-closed eyes (**above** and **right**).*

(Right) *the artist is using a
small bristle brush to lay in
a dark tone for the hair. He
uses thin paint at this stage
so that he can paint over it
at a later stage if necessary.
By starting with relatively
thin paint the artist can
build up the layers of colour
gradually. If you are
working* alla prima *you
will create a thick impasto
immediately, especially if
you are working with a
palette knife. The technique
depends on the directness
and freshness of the
approach — the paint is not
modified after it has been
applied to the canvas.
Impastos can be subtly
changed if necessary by
applying thin glazes.*

*As with all painting it is
important to remember to
return to the subject at
regular intervals. You
should step back from the
painting and spend time
considering it carefully.
Here the artist* **(below)** *is
using a long handled brush
so that he can work at a
distance from the support.
In this way he can see both
the painting and his image
in the mirror at the same
time.*

(Above) *the artist starts to
block in the broad areas of
colour of the clothing. He
works quickly using thin,
easily worked paint. This
blocking-in allows the artist
to assess the painting — are
the main elements of the
painting successfully
arranged within the picture
area? Is it a good
composition? You may, for
instance, decide that you
have included too much of
the background, or too little.
In this case the artist was
particularly concerned
about the position of the
head and whether he should
include more of the torso.
Remember that it is never
too late to change an oil
painting, though obviously
it is easier to make changes
at earlier stages.*

Keep checking the light — if it is from a window you may find that is has changed considerably while you have been absorbed in your work **(right)***. Try to establish the light and dark of the skin tones accurately in relation to each other. It does not matter if the painting looks untidy or if the brushstrokes are visible. These add to the liveliness of the paint surface. These textures are an important element of many paintings — an artist's brushmark can be just as characteristic as handwriting. The detail* **(below)** *shows how exciting a textured paint surface can be.*

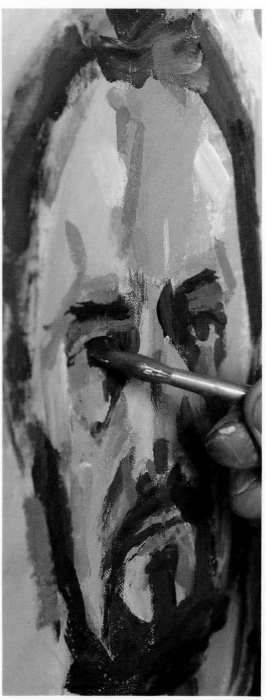

The painter starts to develop the eyes **(above)***. There is a temptation to pay too much attention to them, especially in self-portraits. This is because we concentrate on the eyes when we are talking to people and feel that they reveal the personality. In self-portraits this often results in a strange fixed gaze. The eyes should be described in no greater detail than any other part of the portrait. Here the artist has used broad, simple strokes of paint.*

21

Having laid on the basic skin tones the artist now considers the details: the eyes, nose and mouth. Do not 'draw' these features or paint what you know to be there. Study your face carefully in the mirror and put down what you see, no matter how strange it may seem. Gradually the features will emerge.

*Here the artist is building up the shadows under and around the lids (**above**). and under the nose. By reducing the subject to a series of simple planes — banishing the idea of a face from his mind and perceiving the subject as an abstract the artist will be able to be more objective and therefore more accurate. This is difficult to do when you are painting your own portrait. After all you probably study your own face in the mirror every day of your life and, quite justifiably, feel that you 'know it'.*

*The artist has also worked on the mouth. In the picture at the **top** of the page he is laying in two broad slashes of colour to describe the lips. He uses a lighter tone for the lower lip which catches the light. On the **left** we see that he has established the dark shadow under the lower lip and **above** he has 'knocked back' the brilliant red so that it looks more natural.*

22

The artist studies the painting carefully at this stage and then makes any adjustments which are necessary. **Right** the artist adds touches of darker tone to increase the depth of the shadows. **Below** he adds small areas of subtle tone to complete the shape of the face. **Bottom** he adds final tones to the eyes without making the colours too pronounced. The final picture is simple but convincing — the artist has not attempted to achieve a high degree of finish but has let the paint stand as fairly rough patches of colour. Seen from a distance these colours merge but the broken texture animates the paint surface.

PORTRAIT OF A CHILD

Children's heads contrast strongly with the more sculptured look often found in the heads of adults and therefore deserve special study. In babies, for example, the size of the features are small in relation to the size of the head — and a baby's eyes, nose and mouth are much the same size. The neck which at the earliest stages cannot support the head, remains thin and unstable for quite some time. The way in which the neck enters the cranium is quite different from that in an adult. The cranium is large and grows only slightly after babyhood — and the eyes appear overlarge.

In older children the forehead is curved and appears large due to the small size of the face. The neck is thin, the cheeks full, the chin small and the bridge of the nose is not clearly defined.

The figure of a child is leggy with a protruding tummy, narrow shoulders, and thin arms and legs. All these factors should be reflected in your painting. Even the pose will be different from that of an adult, children tending to adopt upright, rather angular poses.

If you do ask a child to pose remember that their concentration span is short and that they will soon get tired. Allow them frequent breaks and try to make the sessions fun. You will need to make several rapid sketches and you should consider taking photographs. You can refer to these when your young model's patience has run out.

The artist poses his young model, making sure that she is as comfortable as possible **(top)**. *He then selects a hard (H) pencil to make a drawing of the subject directly onto the canvas, putting in the outlines and suggesting the main areas of tone. Using thinly diluted paint the artist starts to block in the dark areas of the girl's hair* **(right)**.

For the darkest skin tones the artist uses raw umber, burnt sienna and black **(centre** *and* **right)**. *He paints the shaded areas of the dress with a mixture of black and cerulean blue, keeping the paint thin and washy* **(above)**. *A mid skin tone is created from black, white and yellow ochre. A touch of cadmium red is added to the lips.*

...is artist mixes his colours ...refully on his palette. ...ch area of tone is painted ...a discrete patch of colour ...th a sharp, clean edge. ...e image gradually begins ...emerge as these facets of ...our build up like the ...ces in a jigsaw. He ...nds back to see how the ...ces are fitting together, ...d makes adjustments as ...cessary (**above** and ...ght).

...re the artist is creating a ...ge of subtly graduated ...es from very few colours ...bove and **right**). ...low he adds the whites ...the eyes using a mixture ...white, yellow ochre and ...ck. The flesh tones begin ...coalesce and the girl's ...tures and the structure of ...r face begins to emerge ...r **right**)..

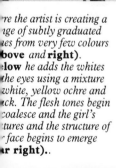

Using the skin tones which he has already mixed on his palette the artist paints in the remaining flesh areas — on the shoulders, neck and arms **(above left** and **right)**. *The picture below shows the contribution this makes to the picture so far.*

The artist uses cerulean blue, black and white to mix a light tone and a darker tone for the girl's blue frock **(right** and **centre)**. *He has already established the darkest areas so he uses these two new shades to block in the remaining areas* **(right)**.

*he artist has blocked in the
...ain areas of blue* **(top
...nd above)**. *He now
...oncentrates on the details
...f the frock using a small
...able brush.* **Top right** *he
... using a mixture of
...erulean blue and black,
...nd for the trimmings
...* **below right)** *he uses
...admium red. He continues
... lay down the paint as
...reas of flat colour with no
...odulation of tone within a
...articular patch of colour.*

The artist mixes a large quantity of white and raw umber for the background. This was applied with broad sweeping movements using a large brush. The artist applied the paint flatly, working up to the outline of the figure, except for an area of white canvas left to stand for highlights on the hair (**above** and **left**).

...ce the background has ...en established the artist ...dies the painting yet ...ain and makes any ...justments necessary ...ft).

The finished painting captures the alert and serious mood of the young model. The large surrounding empty space creates a sense of isolation, drawing attention to her youth and vulnerability. The artist's approach is realistic and he has achieved an excellent likeness, however the way in which he has broken the paint up into areas of flat colour introduces an element of abstraction which adds interest to the painting.

29

GIRL WITH A RED NECKLACE

The approach in this painting contrasts with that in the previous painting — the portrait of a child. There the paint was applied in discrete patches of flat colour. Here the same artist applied thin washes of paint which are built up methodically, each layer being allowed to dry before the next layer is laid over it. The artist started with an accurate and carefully considered drawing. He used only a limited range of colours, exploiting warm and cool colours to describe the form of the features. Cool colours like blues tend in general to recede whilst warm colours like red advance. The artist uses warmer colours on the forehead and the nose, and cooler colours on the turn of the cheek and neck.

The composition also provides us with an interesting contrast with the previous painting. In that case the artist chose to set the figure towards the bottom of the page surrounded by large areas of empty space. In this case, however, he has cropped in to the image so that the girl's head fills the picture area. As a result the painting is more energetic and less contemplative in mood. The painting has been carefully and thoughtfully rendered, but is has, nevertheless a fresh and lively feeling.

or this painting the artist worked from a sketch which he had made from life at an earlier date. He reproduced the image by drawing a faint pencil grid over the sketch. He then made a grid consisting of the same number of squares, on the canvas. He was able to copy the original sketch square by square. You can see the lines of the grid in the picture on the **facing page, (top)**. He used a burnt umber wash to block in the main outlines. Still using thinned paint he blocked in the rest of the subject: gold ochre for the hair, thinned umber for the background and sienna mixed with white for the flesh tones of the face **(bottom left, facing page)**.

In the picture at the **bottom right (facing page)** we see the artist using a flat bristle brush to paint in the darker tones of the hair. This detail shows just how thin the paint is and the way in which the texture of the canvas is revealed through the paint layer.

Using a deeper shade of umber, the artist darkens the background and works up the shadows on the hair and around the eyes **(top right)**. With a mixture of burnt umber and white he then redefines the facial planes, introducing some cadmium red for the warmer areas at the tip of the nose and over the cheek bones **(bottom left)**.
He then mixes a warm flesh tint from burnt sienna, red and white and works over the face, blending the paint and melding the tones. With the handle of his brush he scratches into the paint to create the texture of hair **(bottom right)**.

The artist completes the picture by painting in the necklace using a pure cadmium red. This adds a final touch of bright local colour.